Rumi
Fountain of Fire

A Celebration of Life and Love

Cal-Earth Press
Cal-Earth Institute
Hesperia. California

Cal-Earth Press is the publishing wing of Cal-Earth Institute.

Cal-Earth (California Institute of Earth Art and Architecture) is dedicated to research and education into the universal elements of Earth, Water, Air and Fire, their unity in life - philosophy, poetry, and practice.

Rumi domes of light are designed by architect Nader Khalili and constructed by his apprentices.

Also by the same author:
Racing Alone
Ceramic Houses and Earth Architecture
Sidewalks on the Moon

RUMI, FOUNTAIN OF FIRE
COPYRIGHT © 1994, NADER KHALILI
All Rights Reserved

Printed in the United States of America

For information address:

 Cal-Earth Press
10225 Baldy Lane
Hesperia, CA 92345
email: CalEarth @ AOL.Com

SECOND PRINTING

Library of Congress Catalog Card Number 96-86457

ISBN 1-889625-03-5

Rumi
Fountain of Fire

you are
a sudden resurrection
an endless bliss
you set a fire
in the meadow
of our dreams

laughing today
you are happy
crashing the prisons
blessing the poor

like God Himself
unveiling the sun
spreading hope
bestowing a quest
being the quest
beginning a beginning
setting the end
filling hearts
arranging minds
giving desires
and filling desires

to make a meager living
is not worth the suffering
i let go of preaching
and fill myself with sweets

i set the paper aside
break my pen
name myself silence
i see the cup-bearer is arriving now

come inside the fire

leave your trickery behind
go insane
go mad
burn like a candle-moth

first make yourself a stranger
to yourself and
tear down your house
then move with us
dwell in the abode of love

wash your chest
seven times over
cleansing from hatred
then mold yourself into the chalice
holding the pure wine of love

to understand the intoxicated
you must become intoxicated
to join the eternal soul
you must become a soul

you heard my story and
your spirit grew wings
now you must be annihilated in love
to become a fable of your own

your imagination my friend flies away
then pulls you as a follower
surpass the imagination and
like fate
arrive ahead of yourself

passion and desire
has locked your heart
you must become the key
the teeth of the key
to open all locks

King Solomon gives you a message
listen to the birds
they are talking to you
calling you a trap
frightening them away

to capture us they say
you must make a nest
you must make a nest

your sweetheart's face
is appearing now
change yourself to a mirror
and fill yourself to the brim

so many gifts
you purchased for your love
quit buying gifts
give yourself over

you were a part of the
mineral kingdom in the beginning
then you changed to animal life for awhile
then you found the soul of a human for awhile
now the time has arrived
to become
the soul of souls

come on sweetheart
let's adore one another
before there is no more
of you and me

a mirror tells the truth
look at your grim face
brighten up and cast away
your bitter smile

a generous friend
gives life for a friend
let's rise above this
animalistic behavior
and be kind to one another

spite darkens friendships
why not cast away
malice from our heart

once you think of me
dead and gone
you will make up with me
you will miss me
you may even adore me

why be a worshiper of the dead
think of me as a goner
come and make up now

since you will come
and throw kisses
at my tombstone later
why not give them to me now
this is me
that same person

i may talk too much
but my heart is silence
what else can i do
i am condemned to live this life

the time has come
to break all my promises
tear apart all chains
and cast away all advice

disassemble the heavens
link by link
and break at once
all lovers' ties
with the sword of death

put cotton inside
both my ears
and close them to
all words of wisdom

crash the door and
enter the chamber
where all sweet
things are hidden

how long can i
beg and bargain
for the things of this world
while love is waiting

how long before
i can rise beyond
how i am and
what i am

i am no lion
to overpower my enemies
winning over myself
if i can
is enough

though i'm of lowly earth
since i nourish a seed
named love
i'll grow
lilies of the field

when i'm pitch-black
lamenting separation
i know for sure
i will break through
spreading light on the dark night

i am on fire inside
but look grim outside
since i want to rise
like smoke through my cell

i am a child
whose teacher is love
surely my master
won't let me grow
to be a fool

once again
i broke free of the chains
of the wicked traps
of this world

once again
by your youthful love
i was saved from
this fraud-filled wizard
we call life

non-stop
running day and night
i finally had to cut myself off
from this deadly routine
leaping free as an arrow
from the grip of the cosmic bow

now i have no more fear
of grief and anxiety
i've learned to compete
with death itself

i lived through my wits
for forty years
now at sixty -two
finally hunted down
i am free from struggle

bread becomes blood
blood transforms to milk
and now
that i have my wisdom teeth
i am in no need of more milk

i've come again
like a new year
to crash the gate
of this old prison

i've come again
to break the teeth and claws
of this man-eating
monster we call life

i've come again
to puncture the
glory of the cosmos
who mercilessly
destroys humans

i am the falcon
hunting down the birds
of black omen
before their flights

i gave my word
at the outset to
give my life
with no qualms
i pray to the Lord
to break my back
before i break my word

how do you dare to
let someone like me
intoxicated with love
enter your house

you must know better
if i enter
i'll break all this and
destroy all that

if the sheriff arrives
i'll throw the wine
in his face
if your gatekeeper
pulls my hand
i'll break his arm

if the heavens don't go round
to my heart's desire
i'll crush its wheels and
pull out its roots

you have set up
a colorful table
calling it life and
asked me to your feast
but punish me if
i enjoy myself

what tyranny is this

come and see me

today i am away
out of this world
hidden away
from me and i

i grabbed a dagger
made slices of
me from myself
since i belong
not to me
not to anyone

i am so sorry
for not having done
this cutting away before
it was my soul's mind
and not mine

i have no idea
how my inner fire
is burning today
my tongue
is on a different flame

i see myself
with a hundred faces
and to each one
i swear it is me

surely i must have
a hundred faces
i confess none is mine
i have no face

restless

now i go to the door
now i go on the roof
till i see your face
i'll never know rest

neighbors speak of me
when you are away
as meek or mad
but when you return
everything subsides

this heart of mine
tears itself apart
and seeks no joy
but only wants to know
when you'll arrive

but when you return
and a wine-server is around
i hold a cup
fondle your hair and
caress your face

just come and see me
letting go of my wish
letting go of my pilgrimage
keeping one wish in my heart
making love to your desires

rocks crack apart
filled with passions
longing to have
a glimpse of you

soul grows wings
over-joyed with desire
flying in search of you

fire changes to water
wisdom becomes insanity
and my own eyes
turn out to be the enemy
of my sleep
as they long to see you

there is a dragon
devouring rocks and men
causing insanity
destroying peaceful lives
and calling itself love

please
don't imprison free souls
don't change laughter to cries
don't press us so hard
there is no one
but you to turn to

your love demands
nothing less than
my wounded heart
and my heart is filled
with nothing but your longings

the wine jar is boiling over
someone is drinking the wine
and making the harp play itself
the sonnets to your admiration

your love entered my house
saw me without you
put its hand over my head
and said pity on you

this love journey
is surely the hardest and
most twisted road i have taken
i began the journey but my heart
is still dragging behind
wrapped around your feet

how very close
is your soul with mine
i know for sure
everything you think
goes through my mind

i am with you
now and doomsday
not like a host
caring for you
at a feast alone

with you i am happy
all the times
the time i offer my life
or the time
you gift me your love

offering my life
is a profitable venture
each life i give
you pay in turn
a hundred lives again

in this house
there are a thousand
dead and still souls
making you stay
as this will be yours

a handful of earth
cries aloud
i used to be hair or
i used to be bones

and just the moment
when you are all confused
leaps forth a voice
hold me close
i'm love and
i'm always yours

show me your face
i crave
flowers and gardens

open your lips
i crave
the taste of honey

come out from
behind the clouds
i desire a sunny face

your voice echoed
saying "leave me alone"
i wish to hear your voice
again saying "leave me alone"

i swear this city without you
is a prison
i am dying to get out
to roam in deserts and mountains

i am tired of
flimsy friends and
submissive companions
i die to walk with the brave

i am blue hearing
nagging voices and meek cries
i desire loud music
drunken parties and
wild dances

one hand holding
a cup of wine
one hand caressing your hair
then dancing in orbital circle
that is what i yearn for

i can sing better than any nightingale
but because of
this city's freaks
i seal my lips
while my heart weeps

yesterday the wisest man
holding a lit lantern
in daylight
was searching around town saying

i am tired of
all these beasts and brutes
i seek
a true human

we have all looked
for one but
no one could be found
they said

yes he replied
but my search is
for the one
who cannot be found

only you
i choose
among the entire world

is it fair
of you
letting me be unhappy

my heart
is a pen
in your hand

it is all
up to you
to write me happy or sad

i see only
what you reveal
and live as you say

all my feelings
have the color
you desire to paint

from the beginning
to the end
no one but you

please make
my future
better than the past

when you hide
i change
to a Godless person

and when you
appear
i find my faith

don't expect
to find any more in me
than what you give

don't search for
hidden pockets because
i've shown you that
all i have is all you gave.

i am
the minstrel of
eternal love
and will play
the song of happiness

when my soul
hears music
and changes to softness
i'll break open
the wine jar's seal

i am in love
with the temple of fire
because i was born
as the prophet
named Khalili Abraham

i am in love
with soul and
wisdom
i am the enemy
of false images

the spring is arriving
it is high time
for action
for the sun and Aries
to get together

my blood is boiling
my heart is on fire and
the winter snow
is melting away
from my body

someone's love
is knocking me out
and pulling me
after itself
very forcefully

though i am
in this
hell and fire
i'm filled with
honey and nectar

though i am
condemned to take
this journey
i'm filled with
the sweetness of going home

now the time has come
my sweetheart
kindly express
what my tongue
can never describe

you ask me
who are you and
with such a shaky
existence how can you
fall in love

how do i know
who am i or where i am
how could a single wave
locate itself
in an ocean

you ask me
what am i seeking
above and beyond
the pure light
that i once was

and why am i
imprisoned in this cage
named body and
yet i claim to be
a free bird

how do i know
how i lost my way
i know for sure
i was all straight
before i was
seduced by love

come
let's fall
in love
again

let's turn
all the dirt
in this world
to shiny gold

come
let's be
a new spring
a love reborn

find our aroma
from the essence
of all who
emit heavenly fragrance

like a fresh tree
bloom and spread
all the blessings
right from inside

how long
can i see myself
chained in this prison
chained in this world

the time has come
to take my good life
in my hands and
gallop to the sublime

finally purified
i'm no more polluted
and from now on
i'll take my quests
directly to God Himself

i was given
at my birth
all the estates and mansions
it will be a heresy
to accept only
a doorkeeper's job

once i alter this
doorkeeper's attitude
once i change the
essence in my mind
happiness will replace misery

now my dear heart
since you and i are all alone
having your midnight message
i'll do exactly
that which you know

once i grow wings
in place of my slow feet
all obstacles will vanish
and i really can fly in
time and space again

i've travelled around
raced through every city
while i knew all along
no place could be found
like the city of love

if i could have known
to value what i owned
i would not have suffered
like a fool
the life of a vagabond

i've heard many tunes
all over the globe
all empty
as a kettledrum
except the music of love

it was the sound of
that hollow drum
that made me fall
from the heavens
to this mortal life

i used to soar
among souls
like a heart's flight
winglessly roaming and
celestially happy

i used to drink
like a flower that drinks
without lips or throat
of the wine that overflows
with laughter and joy

suddenly
i was summoned by love
to prepare for a journey
to the temple of
suffering

i cried desperately
i begged and pleaded
and shredded my clothes
not to be sent
to this world

just the way i fear now
going away
to the other world
i was frightened then
to make my descent

love asked me to go
with no fear to be alone
promising to be close
everywhere i go
closer than my veins

love threw its spell
its magic and allure
using coyness and charm
i was totally sold and
bought everything with joy

who am i to resist
love's many tricks
and not to fall
while the whole world
takes love's bait

love showed me
a path but then
lost me on the way
if i could have resisted
i would have found my way

i can show you my friend
surely how you can get there
but here and now
my pen has broken down
before telling you how

i was ready to tell
the story of my life
but the ripple of tears
and the agony of my heart
wouldn't let me

i began to stutter
saying a word here and there
and all along i felt
as tender as a crystal
ready to be shattered

in this stormy sea
we call life
all the big ships
come apart
board by board

how can i survive
riding a lonely
little boat
with no oars
and no arms

my boat did finally break
by the waves
and i broke free
as i tied myself
to a single board

though the panic is gone
i am now offended
why should i be so helpless
rising with one wave
and falling with the next

i don't know
if i am
nonexistence
while i exist
but i know for sure
when i am
i am not
but
when i am not
then i am

now how can i be
a skeptic
about the
resurrection and
coming to life again

since in this world
i have many times
like my own imagination
died and
been born again

that is why
after a long agonizing life
as a hunter
i finally let go and got
hunted down and became free

i was dead
i came alive
i was tears
i became laughter

all because of love
when it arrived
my temporal life
from then on
changed to eternal

love said to me
you are not
crazy enough
you don't
fit this house

i went and
became crazy
crazy enough
to be in chains

love said
you are not
intoxicated enough
you don't
fit the group

i went and
got drunk
drunk enough
to overflow
with light-headedness

love said
you are still
too clever
filled with
imagination and skepticism

i went and
became gullible
and in fright
pulled away
from it all

love said
you are a candle
attracting everyone
gathering every one
around you

i am no more
a candle spreading light
i gather no more crowds
and like smoke
i am all scattered now

love said
you are a teacher
you are a head
and for everyone
you are a leader

i am no more
not a teacher
not a leader
just a servant
to your wishes

love said
you already have
your own wings
i will not give you
more feathers

and then my heart
pulled itself apart
and filled to the brim
with a new light
overflowed with fresh life

now even the heavens
are thankful that
because of love
i have become
the giver of light

all my friends
departed like dreams
left alone
i called upon
one friend
to become
my entire dream

this is the one
who soothes my heart
with endless
tenderness and love

the one who
one hour bestows
inner peace
and the next
the nectar of life

this dream too
as it arrives
i come alive and
as it departs
i'm helpless again

you are drunk
and i'm intoxicated
no one is around
showing us the way home

again and again
i told you
drink less
a cup or two

i know in this city
no one is sober
one is worse than the other
one is frenzied and
the other gone mad

come on my friend
step into the tavern of ruins
taste the sweetness of life
in the company of another friend

here you'll see
at every corner
someone intoxicated
and the cup-bearer
makes her rounds

i went out of my house
a drunkard came to me
someone whose glance
uncovered a hundred
houses in paradise

rocking and rolling
he was a sail
with no anchor but
he was the envy of all those sober ones
remaining on the shore

where are you from i asked
he smiled in mockery and said
one half from the east
one half from the west
one half made of water and earth
one half made of heart and soul
one half staying at the shores and
one half nesting in a pearl

i begged
take me as your friend
i am your next of kin
he said i recognize no kin
among strangers
i left my belongings and
entered this tavern
i only have a chest
full of words
but can't utter
a single one

believe me

i wasn't always like this
lacking common sense
or looking insane

like you
i used to be clever
in my days

never like this
totally enraptured
totally gone

like sharp shooters
i used to be
a hunter of hearts

not like today
with my own heart
drowning in its blood

nonstop asking and
searching for answers
that was then

but now
so deeply enchanted
so deeply enthralled

always pushing
to be ahead and above
since i was not yet hunted down
by this
ever-increasing love

wake up, wake up
this night is gone
wake up

abandon abandon
even your dear self
abandon

there is an idiot
in our market place
selling a precious soul

if you doubt my word
get up this moment
and head for the market now

don't listen to trickery
don't listen to the witches
don't wash blood with blood

first turn yourself upside down
empty yourself like a cup of wine
then fill to the brim with the essence

a voice is descending
from the heavens
a healer is coming

if you desire healing
let yourself fall ill
let yourself fall ill

if you can disentangle
yourself from your selfish self
all heavenly spirits
will stand ready to serve you

if you can finally hunt down
your own beastly self
you have the right
to claim Solomon's kingdom

you are that blessed soul who
belongs to the garden of paradise
is it fair to let yourself
fall apart in a shattered house

you are the bird of happiness
in the magic of existence
what a pity when you let
yourself be chained and caged

but if you can break free
from this dark prison named body
soon you will see
you are the sage and the fountain of life

don't be bitter my friend
you'll regret it soon
hold to your togetherness
or surely you'll scatter

don't walk away gloomy
from this garden
you'll end up like an owl
dwelling in old ruins

face the war and
be a warrior like a lion
or you'll end up like a pet
tucked away in a barn

once you conquer
your selfish self
all your darkness
will change to light

whatever happens
to the world around
show me your purpose
show me your source

even if the world
is Godless and in chaos
show me your anchor
show me your love

if there is hunger
if there is famine
show me your harvest
show me your resource

if life is bitter
everywhere snakes everywhere poison
show me your garden
show me your meadow

if the sun and the moon fall
if darkness rules the world
show me your light
show me your flame

if i have no mouth
or tongue to utter
words of your secrets
show me your fountain

i'll keep silence
how can i express
your life when mine
still is untold

whenever you meet
someone deep drunk
yet full of wisdom
be aware and watch
this person is enthralled
only by love

anytime you see
someone who seems gone
tipsy and happy
filled with rapture
be sure and observe
this is the condition
of someone in love

if you see a head
happy and thrilled
filled with joy
every night and day
this head was fondled
by the fingers of love

every moment
someone is blessed
a tree sprouts
an angel flies
even a monster
leaps with delight

when your body
feels together
when your soul
wants to unite
you are chosen
for a blissful love

rebellious i feel again
i swear i can tear
every chain
you wrap around me

i'm that crazy
fastened fellow who
cages monsters
by his magical tongue

i don't want
this mortal life
i don't desire
this mortal soul

you my life
you my soul
you my love
that's who i want

when you hide away
i feel darkness in my faith
and when you appear
i'm filled with grace

if i drank from this jar
it's because of your reflection
and if i breathe without you
i regret it for the rest of my life

without you i swear
even if i fly
i'm sad
as a dark cloud

without you
even in a rose garden
i feel in prison
i swear again

the music to my ear
is only your name
the dance of my soul
is only with your wine

please come again
and reconstruct
this house of mine
this is my existence

going to an abbey
or going to a mosque
i'm only there
in search of you

running and leaping nonstop
till i catch up
with the fastest rider

annihilating forever
vanishing for good
till i reach the soul of the world

very happy i've become
ever since i changed
to a piece of fire

and with this fire
i'll burn my house and
dwell in the desert

i'll soften and humble
i'll change to earth
till i grow your flowers in me

i'll crawl and flow
i'll change myself to water
till i can reach your paradise garden

without pain no healer
will tend me
or give me potions

i'll change to
total pain
till i get total healing

ever since i was born
i was thrown into this world
helpless and shivering
like a speck of dust in the air

but as soon as i reach
the end of this journey
and settle down
i'll be secured and tranquil forever

every moment
  a voice
  out of this world
  calls on our soul
  to wake up and rise

  this soul of ours
  is like a flame
  with more smoke than light
  blackening our vision
  letting no light through

  lessen the smoke and
  more light brightens your house
  the house you dwell in now
  and the abode
  you'll eventually move to

  now my precious soul
  how long are you going to
  waste yourself
  in this wandering journey
  can't you hear the voice
  can't you use your swifter wings
  and answer the call

if you are a man of this life
then march on this path like a man
or retire and take refuge in your house
since you're not ready for this battle

real men drank a thousand seas and
still died of thirst
you only had a cup
yet boasted of overflowing

you claimed to reach your quest
you'll raise all the dust
yet you've travelled no distance
you've left no mark

now humbly turn to dust
under the gallop of real men
then you'll rise and
become a part of their journey

if you crawl for years
on the path of your quest
do not yield to grief
do not submit to distress

if you can only reflect
like a clean mirror
you'll be that magical spirit

transmute from a wave
to an ocean
from an abyss
to surpass an angel

your soul and mine
used to be mingled
breathing as one
journeying as one

though you're in the limelight now
you must still kiss a candle
to feel the essence
to feel the light

i've come to take you
with me
even if i must drag you along
but first must steal your heart
then settle you in my soul

i've come as a spring
to lay beside your blossoms
to feel the glory of happiness
and spread your flowers around

i've come to show you off
as the adornment of my house
and elevate you to the heavens
as the prayers of those in love

i've come to take back
the kiss you once stole
either return it with grace
or i must take it by force

you're my life
you're my soul
please be my last prayer
my heart must hold you forever

from the lowly earth
to the high human soul
there are a lot more
than a thousand stages

since i've taken you along
from town to town
no way will i abandon
you halfway down this road

though you're in my hands
though i can throw you around
like a child and a ball
i'll always need to chase after you

once again
my sweetheart
found me in town

i was hiding from
love's rapture
i was escaping from the tavern
but soon i was found

what's the use of running
no soul can escape
no use hiding
i've been found a hundred times

i thought i could hide
in a crowded city
how can i when i was found
among my own crowded secrets

now i celebrate with joy
now i'm happy with my luck
just because no matter how
hard i hide i am found

how can i hide
when all over are the marks
spotting the path of
my bleeding hunted heart

and finally my beloved
handed me as i was found
the cup of wine that washes away
all the worries and unhappiness of the world

in every breath
if you're the center
of your own desires
you'll lose the grace
of your beloved

but if in every breath
you blow away
your self claim
the ecstasy of love
will soon arrive

in every breath
if you're the center
of your own thoughts
the sadness of autumn
will fall on you

but if in every breath
you strip naked
just like a winter
the joy of spring
will grow from within

all your impatience
comes from the push
for gain of patience
let go of the effort
and peace will arrive

all your unfulfilled desires
are from your greed
for gain of fulfillments
let go of them all
and they will be sent as gifts

fall in love with
the agony of love
not the ecstasy
then the beloved
will fall in love with you

who is this existence
who puts sadness
in your heart

who is this soul
who sweetens your grief
as soon as you crawl

the one who first frightens you
with deadly snakes
before opening the treasure vault

who changes a monster
to an angel
a sorrow to happiness

who gives the blind
wisdom and
inner sight

who changes darkness
to light
thistles to flowers

who sheds the sins
of the sinful like
autumn leaves

and puts guilt
in the heart of
its own enemies

who makes them
repent and in silence
says amen and
whose amen brings
inner happiness
and soulful delight

who changes bitter thoughts
to lightness and
joyous zeal

bestows fire
and makes you leap
with unknown joy

the fire that can
make a hero
from a desperate heart

who is this existence
who is this
tell me who

if your beloved
has the life of a fire
step in now and burn along

in a night full of
suffering and darkness
be a candle spreading light till dawn

stop this useless
argument and disharmony
show your sweetness and accord

even if you feel
torn to pieces
sew yourself new clothes

your body and soul
will surely feel the joy
when you simply go along

learn this lesson from
lute tambourine and trumpet
learn the harmony of the musicians

if one is playing a wrong note
even among twenty
others will stray out of tune

don't say what is the use
 of me alone being peaceful
when everyone is fighting

you're not one
you're a thousand
just light your lantern

since one live flame
is better than
a thousand dead souls

i swear my dear son
no one in the entire world
is as precious as you are

look at that mirror
take a good look at yourself
who else is there above and beyond you

now give yourself a kiss
and with sweet whispers
fill your ears to the brim

watch for all that beauty
reflecting from you
and sing a love song to your existence

you can never overdo
praising your own soul
you can never over-pamper your heart

you are both
the father and the son
the sugar and the sugar cane

who else but you
please tell me who else
can ever take your place

now give yourself a smile
what is the worth of a diamond
if it doesn't shine

how can i ever put a price
on the diamond that you are
you are the entire treasure of the house

you and your shadow
are forever present in this world
you're that glorious bird of paradise

rocking and rolling
what have you been drinking
please let me know

you must be drunk
going house to house
wandering from street to street

who have you been with
who have you kissed
who's face have you been fondling

you are my soul
you are my life
i swear my life and love is yours

so tell me the truth
where is that fountainhead
the one you've been drinking from

don't hide this secret
lead me to the source
fill my jug over and over again

last night i finally caught
your attention in the crowd
it was your image filling my dream

telling me to stop this wandering
stop this search for
good and evil

i said my dear prophet
give me some of
that you've drunk for ecstasy of life

if i let you drink you said
any of this burning flame
it will scorch your mouth and throat

your portion has been
given already by heaven
ask for more at your peril

i lamented and begged
i desire much more
please show me the source

i have no fear
to burn my mouth and throat
i'm ready to drink every flame and more

the voice of a saviour
will shortly be heard
as soon as you
clear your hearing

don't drink now
this polluted water
the elixir of life
will soon arrive

if you desire grace
lose your selfish self
till you can taste
the sweet essence

in the blackest
of your moments
wait with no fear

since the water of life
was found by the prophet
in the darkest caverns

this time i must confess
i feel a total hate for myself
while crowded and swarmed
my heart wishes to be by single self

seeking that single pearl
i crave to dive deep into this sea
but fear of murderous waves
makes me beg for your help my friends

scattered with so much going on inside
i long for nothing but an inner unity
duality must be abandoned
if you seek to drink the soul of unity

you must bet and lose
everything you've ever owned
if you truly desire
to become one with your beloved

listen to the secret sound
of the revelation now
when your quest aspires the skies
fly away from this lowly earth

my heavenly soul
who only nests in the heights
is tired of its house on earth
it wants to abandon the body
it wants to take the final flight

if you dwell very long
in a heart depressed and dark
be aware you've fallen low
in will and quest

a heart filled with grief
whirling and spinning endlessly
can never feel at peace

what makes you
tremble in fear
that's your true worth now

whatever seems to be
your healing source
is the cause of your pain

whatever you think
is sure secure and forever
is what has hunted you down

whenever your mind flies
it can only land
in the house of madness

whenever love arrives
there is no more space
for your self claim

a heart filled with love
is like a phoenix
that no cage can imprison

such a bird can only fly
above and beyond
any known universe

come let's speak
  of our souls
  let's even hide from
  our ears and eyes

  like a rose garden
  always keep a smile
  like imagination
  talk without a sound

  like the spirit
  reigning the world
  telling the secrets
  uttering no word

  let's get away from
  all the clever humans
  who put words in our mouth
  let's only say what our hearts desire

  even our hands and feet
  sense every inner move
  let's keep silence
  but make our hearts move

  the mystery of destiny
  knows the life of
  speck after speck of dust
  let's tell our story as a particle of dust

if you don't have
enough madness in you
go and rehabilitate yourself

if you've lost a hundred times
the chess game of this life
be prepared to lose one more

if you're the wounded string
of a harp on this stage
play once more then resonate no more

if you're that exhausted bird
fighting a falcon for too long
make a comeback and be strong

you've carved a wooden horse
riding and calling it real
fooling yourself in life

though only a wooden horse
ride it again my friend
and gallop to the next post

you've never really listened
to what God has always
tried to tell you

yet you keep hoping
after your mock prayers
salvation will arrive

your sudden journey
from our city
my beloved
filled you with sweetness
and left me in the dark

you went along
with your own sweetheart
the one for whom
every soul is ready
to leave the body and fly

it was that spectrum
the one who came
first as a light
brightened your path
then took you away in limelight

you were ready
happy to leave this lowly earth
while filled with ecstasy
you flew away with rapture
to the ultimate and beyond

now that you're gone
you've forever found
the ultimate paradise
free from bread
free from bread givers

now you are
like a pure soul
like a dream
every moment
taking a new form

send me some words
of your tender journey
my beloved and
if you don't
i know for sure
you're forever immersed
like a precious pearl
in the endless sea

i want to leave this town
but you've chained me down
stolen away my heart
leaving yourself behind

now i've lost my way
my soul restless and head twisted
all because of those secrets
you once whispered

i only must keep
fasting my heart
to set me free
from sleepless nights

since your only advice
when you saw me in flame
was to keep burning
with you or with your thoughts

words of wisdom
came to me at last
"the beloved you've lost
the one you've been seeking outside
can only be found inside"

you mustn't be afraid of death

you're a deathless soul
you can't be kept in a dark grave
you're filled with God's glow

be happy with your beloved
you can't find any better
the world will shimmer
because of the diamond you hold

when your heart is immersed
in this blissful love
you can easily endure
any bitter face around

in the absence of malice
there is nothing but
happiness and good times
don't dwell in sorrow my friend

look what have you done
hunted my heart
hunted my soul
but left them behind

you raptured my life
broke my cage
but wounded my heart
then wished to depart

though i know your wish
though i suffer the separation
i have no courage to ask
what have you done

i know why a candle burns
i know why a candle cries
since you're the cause
of pulling its life apart

i know why a harp
bows as it is played
since like a slave
you made it bend to obey

with all the tyranny you caused
as soon as i see your face
my poisoned life turns sweet
my pain is perfectly healed

every leaf in hope
holds its palm open
begging for more
knowing your endless bliss

i'm not going to leave
this house and set out
on a journey any more
i've everything right here

in every corner
a garden of memories
devoid of darkness
devoid of fear

the news of my journey
spreading in this town
is but a rumor of envy
sent around by the enemy

how can i think
of going very far
how can i walk headless
how can i go with no soul

how can i ever find
anywhere in this world
a more beautiful face
a more desired beloved

even the moon
is seeking for this love
to see its reflection
to find its adornment

if i ever talk about
going to travel
or leaving this town
break my teeth with no qualms

i've lost my feet
going to the sea of love
but like a boat
i need no feet to crawl

and even if you
throw me out of your door
i'll come back
through the roof hole

because of your love
i'll be dancing and floating
in this air as a speck of dust
to finally settle into your house

where have you gone
the settler of my soul
did you fly away
or hide in your home

as soon as you saw
the loyalty of my heart
you turned around and
flew like a bird

your vision captured
the wandering of our spirits
then away from the crowd
you journeyed in solitude

you went away so quick
as though you were
a morning breath
carrying a flower's aroma

but you really didn't fly away
as a bird or a breeze
you were created from God's light
you went immersed in His glow

come down my love

abandon your adventurous flight
it's high time for a happy life

come into my house
throw out my old belongings
burn me again with your love

i know for sure
even if you burn the entire house
your love will build me a new paradise

you empowered the drops of water
to shine like diamonds
you blew life into a piece of clay

you gave a lowly fly
the same wings as an eagle
the aspiration of the sky

there was a blind sage in our town
a healer took mercy on him with medicine
to set his eyes open to the light

the sage refused and replied
if you could only see the light i see
you'd pluck out both of your eyes

my secret beloved
sent me a secret message

"give me your soul
give me your life

wander like a drifter
go on a journey

walk into this fire with grace
be like a salamander

come into our source of flame
fire transmutes to a rose garden

don't you know that my thorn
is better than the queen of roses

don't you know my heresy
is the essence of spirituality

then surrender your spirit
surrender your life"

oh God i know
a garden is better than a cage

i know a palace
is better than a ruin

but i'm that owl in this world
who loves to live in the ruins of love

i may be that poor wandering soul
but watch all the aspiration and light

watch the glow of God
reflecting from my face

my dear heart
you're a fire worshiper
an explosive in flame

call on the cupbearer
to sprinkle the wine on you
to soothe your burn with water

that special cupbearer
the same one who sizzles
lives with wine and lips with kisses

the one who first calmed my mind
gave me a cup of fiery wine
and took me to a secret house

in that special house
dwelled a precious sweetheart
who offered me a choice

a tray full of gold
a tray full of flame
a few words i was told

this gold is soaked with fire
this fire is filled with gold
if you choose fire you'll end up with gold

if you choose the burden of gold
you'll lay heavy and cold
take the fire of the beloved and leap with joy

i'm loyal
to the image and beauty
of my beloved
please speak of that image only
and say no more

whenever you're with me
speak only about
the generosity of candles
the generosity of the sugarcane
and say no more

don't speak of any suffering
show me the treasure that waits
at the end of the road
if you're ignorant of the path
then say no more

last night i was in flame
my beloved saw me and said
"i'm here at last
don't tear your clothes
lament no more"

i begged my beloved
to understand my condition
to sense my fear
my love said "when i'm present
you must seek no more

i'll whisper the words
of secrets into your ear
and you must promise not to answer
just nod your head
and say no more

the face of a sweetheart
has penetrated your heart
the tenderness is all there is
your journey is the journey of love
sense it to the depth and say no more"

i asked if the face
belongs to a human
or that of an angel
"neither this nor that
sense it but say no more"

i said if you don't
identify this for me at once
my life will be shattered
"be shattered at once
but say no more

you're dwelling in
a house filled with
images and dreams
pack all your belongings
move out but say no more"

you're simply expressing
the experience of God
i said to the beloved
"yes this is the answer
but for God's sake say no more"

haven't i told you
don't run away from me
you'll find me like a fountainhead
wherever you go in this mirage

even if you leave me
with anger for a hundred thousand years
you'll finally return
since i'm your final home

haven't i told you
don't be fooled with
the spangles in life
i'm your final fulfillment

haven't i told you
that i'm the sea and you're a small fish
you're better off staying with me
than venturing the dry shores

haven't i told you
don't go towards the trap
like a bird enticed by bait
come back to me i'm your endless strength

haven't i told you
others will kill your fire
stay with me who will set you
on flame and warm your soul

haven't i told you
others will disillusion you
you'll lose the fountainhead of
the solace i've found for you

if you're enlightened by
the lantern of your heart
guiding you to God's house
look at me i may be the path

look at love
how it tangles
with the one fallen in love

look at spirit
how it fuses with earth
giving it new life

why are you so busy
with this or that or good or bad
pay attention to how things blend

why talk about all
the known and the unknown
see how unknown merges into the known

why think separately
of this life and the next
when one is born from the last

look at your heart and tongue
one feels but deaf and dumb
the other speaks in words and signs

look at water and fire
earth and wind
enemies and friends all at once

the wolf and the lamb
the lion and the deer
far away yet together

look at the unity of this
spring and winter
manifested in the equinox

you too must mingle my friends
since the earth and the sky
are mingled just for you and me

be like sugarcane
sweet yet silent
don't get mixed up with bitter words

my beloved grows
right out of my own heart
how much more union can there be

find yourself a friend
who is willing to
tolerate you with patience

put to the test the essence
of the best incense
by putting it in fire

drink a cup of poison
if handed to you by a friend
when filled with love and grace

step into the fire
like the chosen prophet
the secret love will change
hot flames to a garden
covered with blossoms
roses and hyacinths and willow

spinning and throwing you
a true friend can hold you
like God and His universe

don't tell me i had enough
don't stop me from having more
my soul isn't yet satisfied

last night an intoxicated friend
handed me his wine jar
i broke the jar in spite of my desire

i'm not enslaved
by my craving body
i'll not pollute this endless longing

i've broken the barriers
of the past and the future
without being drunk

love's message came to me this morning
hiding itself as a healer
taking my pulse and declaring i'm weak

"don't drink wine
given by anyone
but your beloved"

if i can only find i said
the fountainhead named love
what use is any wine

my dear friend
never lose hope
when the beloved
sends you away

if you're abandoned
if you're left hopeless
tomorrow for sure
you'll be called again

if the door is shut
right in your face
keep waiting with patience
don't leave right away

seeing your patience
your love will soon
summon you with grace
raise you like a champion

and if all the roads
end up in dead ends
you'll be shown the secret paths
no one will comprehend

the beloved i know
will give with no qualms
to a puny ant
the kingdom of Solomon

my heart has journeyed
many times around the world
but has never found
and will never find
such a beloved again

ah i better keep silence
i know this endless love
will surely arrive
for you and you and you

one by one
our friends
filled with joy and quest
begin to arrive

one by one our friends
the worshipers of ecstasy
begin to arrive

more friends and sweethearts
filling you with love
are on their way

darlings of spring
journeying from gardens
begin to arrive

one by one
living their destiny
in this world

the ones who are gone are gone
but the ones who survived
begin to arrive

all their pockets
filled with gold
from endless treasures

bringing gifts
for the needy of the world
begin to arrive

the weak and the exhausted
the frightened by love
will be gone

the rejuvenated
the healthy and happy
begin to arrive

the pure souls
like the spectrums
of the shining sun

descending from the high heavens
to lowly earth
begin to arrive

luscious and happy
the blessed garden
whose heavenly fruits

spring forth
from the virgin winter
begin to arrive

those who are born
from the roots
of generosity and love

taking a journey
from paradise to paradise
begin to arrive

how long will you hide
your beautiful
festive smile

teach your laughter
to a flower
manifest an eternity

why do you think
the door to the sky
is closed on your face

it allures and invites
your magical touch
to open and arrive

an entire caravan
is waiting in ecstasy
for your coming and leading

come on my friend
use your talisman and
harness all their souls

today is the day to unite
with your longing beloved
wait no more
for an unknown tomorrow

a tambourine is in a corner
begging your playing hands
a flute is sitting dormant
begging your happy lips

where did it all go
the dancing the love and the music
could it be that none was there
or it was but all
went to the vanishing point

it is better not to be skeptic
look at Moses' magic cane
one minute a cane the next a dragon

or was it a dragon first
and as it devoured the world
within its existence
it changed to a cane

every situation is
like an arrow
when it is gone my friend
seek and find it in the target

though a pearl
has stolen a grain of sand
from the nearby shore
a wise diver will seek it out
in the depth of the ocean floor

if you stay awake
for an entire night
watch out for a treasure
trying to arrive

you can keep warm
by the secret sun of the night
keeping you eyes open
for the softness of dawn

try it for tonight
challenge your sleepy eyes
do not lay your head down
wait for heavenly alms

night is the bringer of gifts
Moses went on a ten-year journey
during a single night
invited by a tree
to watch the fire and light

Mohammed too made his passage
during that holy night
when he heard the glorious voice
when he ascended to the sky

day is to make a living
night is only for love
commoners sleep fast
lovers whisper to God all night

all night long
a voice calls upon you
to wake up
in the precious hours

if you miss your chance now
when your body is left behind
your soul will lament
death is a life of no return

if you can't go to sleep
my dear soul
for tonight
what do you think will happen

if you pass your night
and merge it with dawn
for the sake of heart
what do you think will happen

if the entire world
is covered with the blossoms
you have labored to plant
what do you think will happen

if the elixir of life
that has been hidden in the dark
fills the desert and towns
what do you think will happen

if because of
your generosity and love
a few humans find their lives
what do you think will happen

if you pour an entire jar
filled with joyous wine
on the head of those already drunk
what do you think will happen

go my friend
bestow your love
even on your enemies
if you touch their hearts
what do you think will happen

everywhere
the aroma of God
begins to arrive

look at these people
not knowing their feet from head
as they begin to arrive

every soul is seeking His soul
every soul parched with thirst
they've all heard the voice
of the quencher of thirst

everyone tastes the love
everyone tastes the milk
anxious to know
from where the real mother
begins to arrive

waiting in fever
wondering ceaselessly
when will that final union
begin to arrive

Moslems and Christians and Jews
raising their hands to the sky
their chanting voice in unison
begin to arrive

how happy is the one
whose heart's ear
hears that special voice
as it begins to arrive

clear your ears my friend
from all impurity
a polluted ear
can never hear the sound
as it begins to arrive

if your eyes are marred
with petty visions
wash them with tears
your teardrops are healers
as they begin to arrive

keep silence
don't rush to finish your poem
tthe finisher of the poem
he creator of the word
will begin to arrive

how long should i bear
this distressed life
because of hopes and fears

give me some wine
rescue me for a while
from these hopes and fears

hand me that cup
that flaming cup
the one that burns away

all those piled up thoughts
filling my brain
with hopes and fears

pour into my throat
whatever has been
my share of life

don't make me wait forever
like a knocker on a door
with hopes and fears

give me a sip
of that water of life
to attain my inner spectrum

these moments i feel
i've lost all my colors
because of hopes and fears

give me that fiery water
the one that even
the elixir wishes for

i crave forever more
the promised paradise
with hopes and fears

you are forever
my shining sun and
i am like this poem
restless with hopes and fears

if you distance yourself
only for an hour
from your endless thoughts
what do you think will happen

if you let yourself sink
just like a fish
into the ocean of our love
what do you think will happen

you are merely
a piece of straw
and we are
that eternal amber

if you leap forth
from your lowly house
to fuse with the amber
what do you think will happen

a hundred times
you've promised yourself
to depart from self-claim
to be humble as earth

only for once
if you keep your word
what do you think will happen

you're a precious
hidden diamond
sunken in the mud

if you wash away
all that impurity
from your gorgeous face
what do you think will happen

if you abandon
for a little while
your ego and greed
tear down your shield
rise with a quest
to unite with the divine
what do you think will happen

i don't need
a companion who is
nasty sad and sour

the one who is
like a grave
dark depressing and bitter

a sweetheart is a mirror
a friend a delicious cake
it isn't worth spending
an hour with anyone else

a companion who is
in love only with the self
has five distinct characters

stone hearted
unsure of every step
lazy and disinterested
keeping a poisonous face

the more this companion waits around
the more bitter everything will get
just like a vinegar
getting more sour with time

enough is said about
sour and bitter faces
a heart filled with desire for
sweetness and tender souls
must not waste itself with unsavory matters

come come come
my endless desires
come come come

come my beloved
come my sweetheart
come come come

don't talk about the journey
say no more
of the path one must take

you are my path
you are my journey
come come come

you stole from this earth
a bouquet of roses
i am hidden in that bouquet
come come come

as long as i am sober
and keep talking about
good and bad
i'm missing
the most important event
seeing your face
come come come

i must be a moron
missing this life
if i don't cast my mind
in the fire of your love
come come come

come on darling
pass me one more cup
bestow on my soul
tranquility once more

and do it now
today is my turn
i can wait no more
for the unknown tomorrow

if you have as my share
even a small trace of grace
give it to me now
don't make me wait

let me go free
help me to break out
from this new trap
i've fallen into again

don't hand me over
to the monster of my thoughts
my thoughts are another trap
another waiting vampire

take my only belongings
take them to the pawn shop
pledge them once more and
bring me the last cup

how long
can i lament
with this depressed
heart and soul

how long
can i remain
a sad autumn
ever since my grief
has shed my leaves

the entire space
of my soul
is burning in agony

how long can i
hide the flames
wanting to rise
out of this fire

how long can one suffer
the pain of hatred
of another human
a friend behaving like an enemy

with a broken heart
how much more
can i take the message
from body to soul

i believe in love
i swear by love
believe me my love

how long
like a prisoner of grief
can i beg for mercy

you know i'm not
a piece of rock or steel
but hearing my story
even water will become
as tense as a stone

if i can only recount
the story of my life
right out of my body
flames will grow

don't go to sleep
this night
one night is worth
a hundred thousand souls

the night is generous
it can give you
a gift of the full moon
it can bless your soul
with endless treasure

every night when you feel
the world is unjust
never ending grace
descends from the sky
to soothe your souls

the night is not crowded like the day
the night is filled with eternal love
take this night
tight in your arms
as you hold a sweetheart

remember the water of life
is in the dark caverns
don't be like a big fish
stopping the life's flow
by standing in the mouth of a creek

even Mecca is adorned
with black clothes
showing that the heavens
are ready to grace
the human soul

even one prayer
in the Mecca of a night
is like a hundred
no one can claim
sleep can build
a temple like this

during a night
the blessed prophet
broke all the idols and
God remained alone
to give equally to all
an endless love

a voice out of this world
calls on our souls
not to wait any more
get ready to move
to the original home

your real home
your real birth place
is up here with the heavens
let your soul take a flight
like a happy phoenix

you've been tied up
your feet in the mud
your body roped to a log
break loose your ties
get ready for the final flight

make your last journey
from this strange world
soar for the heights
where there is no more
separation of you and your home

God has created
your wings not to be dormant
as long as you are alive
you must try more and more
to use your wings to show you're alive

these wings of yours
are filled with quests and hopes
if they are not used
they will wither away
they will soon decay

you may not like
what i'm going to tell you
you are stuck
now you must seek
nothing but the source

when i die
when my coffin
is being taken out
you must never think
i am missing this world

don't shed any tears
don't lament or
feel sorry
i'm not falling
into a monster's abyss

when you see
my corpse is being carried
don't cry for my leaving
i'm not leaving
i'm arriving at eternal love

when you leave me
in the grave
don't say goodbye
remember a grave is
only a curtain
for the paradise behind

you'll only see me
descending into a grave
now watch me rise
how can there be an end
when the sun sets or
the moon goes down

it looks like the end
it seems like a sunset
but in reality it is a dawn
when the grave locks you up
that is when your soul is freed

have you ever seen
a seed fallen to earth
not rise with a new life
why should you doubt the rise
of a seed named human

have you ever seen
a bucket lowered into a well
coming back empty
why lament for a soul
when it can come back
like Joseph from the well

when for the last time
you close your mouth
your words and soul
will belong to the world of
no place no time

DREAMS OF RUMI

Rumi's poems, in Persian, have been whispered in my ears for over fifty years. The endless ocean of his sixty-five thousand couplet-verses have blessed my own creative work, letting me search for fire in its tranquil waters for two decades. And I have been graced by his visit in my dreams which bestowed on me enough courage to enter his words:

In my dream Rumi is standing in the street, next to the curb, with several companions. The young and jovial Rumi, is about twenty-eight, round-faced, with a full head of curlicue hair. He is wearing a blue-grey suit and a white shirt with the last button undone, and is a firm, healthy five-foot-five, looking younger than his age. His smile is surely the most striking feature of his physical presence. A smile brimming with quest, humbleness, victory, needlessness, and love.

I smile at him. I am standing on the sidewalk, desperately wanting to go forward to meet him, but the man next to him is my enemy. This man is young Rumi's guide for the tour of our city. He is the only man I have known in my life who hates me as much as I once hated him. Thus my meeting Rumi seems impossible. Until seconds later, when in my dream I declare to my heart and God that I am ready to go and beg my enemy's pardon, just so that I can have a chance to meet Rumi. No sooner do I make this wish than I find Rumi sitting next to me.

We are kneeling next to a low table, on adjoining sides, and looking at a large paper filled with Persian calligraphy. All along I keep looking at his face, at his smile, and feel more at ease in my body and soul. I lower my head with shyness and say:

"These are your poems. I have calligraphed all my favorite ones on this paper."

He looks at them for a long time, then takes the pen from my hand, and right in the middle of the paper, over a couple of the Persian words adds three or four missing dots. He then smiles and says, "Ah, these poems!"

I look at him, smile , and say, "But the verse I love the best is not here."

"What verse is that?"

"Aab kam ju teshnegi aavar bedast, seek not water, seek thirst."

He smiles and says, "That one is my favorite one too."

And I wake up.

A year later, ever more enraptured with his poems in my Archemy (architecture and alchemy) work for designing colonies on the moon and Mars, I am still unsure how I can ever begin translating some of them into English. Then I have another dream:

I dream I am walking in a dry river bed. I come to the end and see a dam. A high dam created by a hill of fist-sized rocks. All the rocks are darker than ebony. I stand there, look up at the very steep dam and say, 'Ah, how high! Who can climb this?' No sooner do I utter these words when I hear a voice,

Rumi's voice, in Persian, from behind coming to my ear. 'Boro baalaa Yaadet baasheh, hameh-e in sang-haa talaast., Go up. Remember, all these rocks are gold.' "

Two years later, on a special day, some verses of the first poem begin to appear in a free-spirited way. And continues since, distilling, mostly in the slice of two-to-four in the morning. The sequence of these selected poems from the Di*wan-i Shams-i Tabrizi* follows the water and fire of my own soul, the agony and the delicious insomnia of my own life in a big city.

—*Nader Khalili*

The primary language of Islamic civilization is Arabic, a Semitic language closely akin to Hebrew. When Muslim scholars wanted to write on Koran commentary, Hadith, jurisprudence, theology, philosophy, and theoretical Sufism, they normally chose Arabic. But Arabic remained the exclusive language of Islamic learning only in the Arabic-speaking countries, which make up a relatively small proportion of the Islamic world. In many other countries, the vernacular languages also made important contributions. This is especially true of Iran, the home of the Persian language, which belongs to the Indo-European group and is therefore related to English.

Like modern science, the Islamic sciences have always been the domain of an elite, a group who are known as the "ulama" (the "learned" or the "possessors of knowledge"). Few people become ulama. Most gained enough knowledge about their religion to practice it, but they never studied such fields of learning as Koran commentary, Hadith, theology, or philosophy. Nevertheless, the Islamic world view became deeply rooted in all levels of society. To a large degree this occurred because of the all-pervasive influence of poetry, which expressed the learned culture in popular language to a degree unimaginable in the modern world. Practically all traditional Muslims, even the illiterate, appreciate poetry, and many of them know reams of it by heart. And the most popular poetry, especially in the Persian context, has always been the best poetry, which is to say that it was written by the greatest poets of the Persian language. All these poets embodied Islamic culture and learning, and many were not only good Muslims, but also Sufi masters of great spiritual accomplishment.

As soon as the modern Persian language took its present form in about the tenth century, it spread outside Iran and gradually became a language of religious significance. In the Indian subcontinent, Persian surpassed Arabic to become the primary language of Islamic learning, and it also played a highly significant cultural and religious role in Turkey. Probably the most important reason for Persian's spread was the extraordinary beauty and attractiveness of its poetry. Few if any other languages of the world have produced as many great poets as Persian. If relatively few of these poets have become known in the West, this is primarily because it is extremely difficult to provide satisfactory (not to speak of good) translation of their works. Umar Khayyam became famous in the West not because he was a first rate poet, but because Edward Fitzgerald was able to strike a chord with the English-reading public through his verse renderings (however inaccurate these may be).

Most Persian speakers would agree that the greatest of all Persian poets is Hafiz, but translators have been singularly unsuccessful in rendering his verses into English. Although a relatively large number of talented people have taken up Hafiz's challenge, the grace, beauty, and content of his poetry is too intimately bound up with the imagery and sound of Persian language to allow for much more than a caricature.

In the modern West, Jalaloddin Rumi has become the best known Persian poet. Some Persian speakers may consider him the greatest poet of their language, but not if they are asked to stress the verbal perfections of the verses rather than the meaning that the words convey. Rumi's success in the West has to do with the fact that his message transcends the limitation of language. He has something important to say, and he says it in a way that is not completely bound up with the intricacies and beauty of the Persian language and the culture which that language conveys, nor even with poetry (he is also the author of prose works, including his *Discourses,* available in a good English translation by A.J. Arberry). One does not have to appreciate poetry to realize that Rumi is one of the greatest spiritual teachers who ever lived.

Rumi's greatness has to do with the fact that he brings out what he calls "the roots of the roots of the roots of the religion," or the most essential message of Islam, which is the most essential message of traditional religion everywhere: Human beings were born for unlimited freedom and infinite bliss, and their birthright is within their grasp. But in order to reach it, they must surrender to love. What makes Rumi's expression of this message different from other expressions is his extraordinary directness and uncanny ability to employ images drawn from everyday life.

The story of Rumi's career has often been told.* He was born in Balkh, in present-day Afghanistan, in the year 1204. His father, Baha Walad, was a well-known scholar and Sufi and the author of a fascinating collection of meditations on the intimacy of divine love. Baha Walad took his family to Anatolia in about 1220, when the impending Mongol invasion made it dangerous to remain in eastern Iran. He settled in Konya in present-day Turkey, where he continued his career as one of the best known ulama of the time. When he died in 1231, his son Jalaloddin became his successor. Before long Jalaloddin was recognized as a great professor and preacher. He combined studies of the legal and theological sciences with the more inward and spiritual orientation of Sufism, but he was not yet known as an authority in the Sufi sciences, nor did he compose poetry.

The great transformation in Rumi's life began in 1244, when he was forty (in Islamic lore, forty is the age of spiritual maturity and also of prophecy; the angel Gabriel appeared to Muhammad for the

first time when he was forty). In this year
an enigmatic figure called Shams al-Din
of Tabriz, or Shams-i Tabrizi, appeared in
Konya. He and Rumi quickly became
inseparable. Shams seems to have opened
Rumi up to certain dimensions of the
mysteries of divine love that he had not
yet experienced. For Rumi Shams became
the embodiment of God's beauty and
gentleness, the outward mark of His
guiding mercy. Their closeness led some
of Rumi's students and disciples to become
jealous, and eventually Shams
disappeared. Some whispered that he had
been murdered, but Rumi himself does
not seem to have believed the rumors.
What is clear is that Shams's disappearance
was the catalyst for Rumi's extraordinary
outpouring of poetry. Rumi makes this
point explicit in many passages. He
alludes to it in the first line of his great
Mathnawi, where he says,

> "Listen to this reed as it tells its tale,
> complaining of separations."

For Rumi, separation from Shams was
the outward sign of separation from God,
which is only half the story. As much as
Rumi complains of separation, he

celebrates the joys of union. Shams, he lets us know, never really left him, nor was Rumi ever truly separate from God.

"Shamsi-i Tabrizi is but a pretext—
I display the beauty of God's gentleness, I !"

Rumi wrote about 3,000 ghazals (love poems), signing many of them with Shams's name. This explains the title of his collected ghazals and miscellaneous verse, *Diwan-i shams-i Tabrizi,* which includes about 40,000 lines. His other great collection of poems, the 25,000-verse *Mathnawi,* was composed as a single work with a didactic aim. R.A. Nicholson rendered a great service to the English-reading public by translating it in its entirety. But relatively few of the *Diwan's* nuggets have been mined. Nicholson published a number of ghazals in 1898 and A.J. Arberry retranslated these and added many more, for a total of 400. I translated seventy-five ghazals and a thousand scattered verses in my *Sufi Path of Love.*

More recently, a number of poets have undertaken to publish some of the gems of the *Diwan* while trying to preserve the poetical quality in English, usually basing themselves on literal translations done by others. For those who read Persian, most of these versions have been rather pale, and frequently inaccurate. But one has to thank all such devotees of Rumi for recognizing that he deserves to be more widely known and for attempting to make his poetry available in readable and attractive versions.

I have looked at most of the collections of translations from Rumi's *Diwan* and have been most pleased by those of my friend Nader Khalili, found in the present volume. Nader has the advantage over most translators of being a native speaker of Persian. He also has a natural artistic gift that appears in various dimensions of his work. His book *Racing Alone,* although written in prose, is a profoundly poetical account of the quest for beauty and perfection that fills his life and becomes manifest visually in his architecture (see his *Ceramic Houses & Earth Architecture).* In contrast to most of those attracted to Rumi today, Nader has been able to bring out the fact that Rumi's message has a practical and concrete relevance to our everyday world. Beauty, Rumi knows, is a profound need of the human soul, because God is beautiful and the source of all beauty, and God is the soul's only real need. Nader has been performing a major human service by bringing beauty into architectural forms. In this volume he illustrates his versatility by bringing it into linguistic forms as well.

Professor William C. Chittick
State University of New York, Stony Brook,
21 June 1992

* For Rumi's life and work see Annemarie Schimmel, *I Am Wind, You Are Fire: The Life and Work of Rumi* (Boston: Shambhala, 1992); idem, *The Triumphal Sun: A Study of the Works of Jalaloddin Rumi* (London: East-West publications, 1978); William C. Chittick, *The Sufi Path of Love: The Spiritual Teachings of Rumi* (Albany: SUNY Press, 1983); idem, *"Rumi and the Mawlawiyya,"* in S.H. Nasr (ed.), *Islamic Spirituality: Manifestations* (New York: Crossroad, 1991), pp. 105-126

NOTE ON TRANSLATION

The translation of these "Ghazals" love poems from the book of the Diwan-i Shams-i Tabrizi are taken from the Furuzanfar's tenth Persian edition.

The poems correspond with the Furuzanfar's numbered Ghazals and are listed in the index. I have presented these poems according to the date of their translation as they came to me. Searching and choosing of these specific poems corresponds with the events of my life, and the dreams of the time.

Also by Nader Khalili...

Racing Alone
Ceramic Houses and Earth Architecture
Sidewalks on the Moon

INDEX

if you can disentangle yourself 45; 3291; 12/4/91
if you can only reflect 56; 3264; 1/4/92
if you can't go to sleep 106; 838; 4/16/92
if you distance yourself 112; 844; 4/19/92
if you don't have enough madness in you 75; 1194; 2/13/92
if you dwell very long 72; 609; 2/3/92
if you stay awake 104; 258; 4/13/92
if your beloved 64; 1197; 1/18/92
I'm loyal to the image and beauty 90; 2219; 3/1/92
I'm not going to leave 82; 2614; 2/16/92
in every breath 60; 323; 1/12/92
i've come again like a new year 14; 1375; 3/17/91
I've come to take you with me 57; 322; 1/12/92
I've travelled around 32; 1509; 4/8/91
look at love 94; 2381; 3/9/92
look what have you done 80; 2589; 2/16/92
my dear friend 98; 965; 3/28/92
my dear heart you're a fire worshiper 88; 2523; 2/25/92
my secret beloved sent me a secret message 86; 2508; 2/25/92
once again i broke free of the chains 12; 1472; 3/17/91
once again my sweetheart 59; 330; 1/12/91
one by one our friends 100; 891; 3/29/92
only you i choose 24; 1521; 4/91
rebellious i feel again 50; 2162; 12/21/91
restless now i go to the door 17; 1512; 3/91
rocking and rolling 68; 2154; 1/19/92
rocks crack apart 18; 2157; 3/91
running and leaping non-stop 52; 1400; 12/28/91
show me your face 22; 441; 3/91
the time has come to break all my promises 10; 1591; 3/6/91
the voice of a saviour will shortly be heard 70; 550; 1/18/92
this time i must confess 71; 3210; 1/27/92
wake up, wake up 44; 2133; 11/23/91
whatever happens to the world around 47; 2144; 12/21/91